GLADIATORS AND EMPERORS: A KIDS' GUIDE TO THE ROMAN EMPIRE

Medina Books

Table of Contents

01

INTRODUC TION

Overview of the Roman Empire

Welcome to Gladiators and Emperors: A Kids' Guide to the Roman Empire! In this guide, we will take a look at the history of the Roman Empire and its many aspects. The Roman Empire was one of the largest and most influential empires of its time, ruling much of Europe and parts of North Africa and the Middle East.

The Roman Empire was founded in 27 BC by Augustus Caesar and lasted until 476 AD. At its height, the Roman Empire was the largest political entity in the world, ruling over an area of 2.5 million square miles (6.5 million square kilometers). The population of the Roman Empire was estimated to be around 50 million people.

The Roman Empire was divided into two parts, the Western Roman Empire and the Eastern Roman Empire. The Western Roman Empire was made up of Italy, Gaul, Spain, and parts of North Africa. The Eastern Roman Empire was made up of Greece, Anatolia (modern-day Turkey), Syria, and parts of the Middle East.

The Roman Empire was a powerful and influential civilization, known for its engineering, architecture, and art. The Romans were also known for their military prowess, having won many battles and wars.

The Roman Empire was a monarchy and was ruled by an emperor. The emperor was responsible for making laws and keeping order in the empire. The emperor had a council of advisors called the Senate who assisted him in making decisions. The emperor was usually able to choose his successor, although there were often disputes between family members and rival political factions.

The Roman Empire was a very successful civilization, due to its strong government, military, and economy. The Roman Empire also had a form of currency, called the denarius, which helped fuel its economy. Trade was also an important part of the Roman Empire, with goods being traded all over the world.

The Roman Empire was also a center of culture, with literature, art, and architecture flourishing in its cities. The Colosseum in Rome is a famous example of the Roman Empire's art and architecture.

The Roman Empire was an incredibly powerful and influential civilization, with its culture and legacy still influencing the world today. We hope this guide will help you learn more about the Roman Empire and its many aspects.

Why is the Roman Empire Important to Study?

The Roman Empire is one of the most fascinating and influential civilizations in the history of the world. It is important to study the Roman Empire because it shaped the world in many ways, both politically and culturally.

The Roman Empire was founded in 753 BC and lasted until 476 AD. During this time, it was one of the most powerful empires in the world, with an area stretching from Britain to the Middle East. The Roman Empire left its mark on many aspects of life, from its laws and government to its art and architecture.

The Roman Empire also had a major influence on language. Latin, the language of the Romans, was spoken throughout the empire and is still used in many countries today. Latin was the basis for many European languages, including French, Spanish, and Italian.

The Romans also introduced many concepts that are still used today, such as the twelve-month calendar, the idea of democracy, and the concept of citizenship. Roman law was based on principles of justice and fairness, and is still used in many countries today.

The Roman Empire also gave us many of the sports we enjoy today. Gladiatorial combat was a popular form of entertainment in the Roman Empire, and modern sports such as boxing and wrestling can trace their origins back to these ancient contests.

The Romans were also famous for their engineering feats. The Roman aqueducts, the Colosseum, and the Pantheon were all major engineering projects that were built during the Roman Empire.

The Roman Empire is important to study because it shaped the world in so many ways. Its influence can still be seen today, and understanding the history of the Roman Empire can help us better understand our own society and culture.

02

THE FOUNDING OF ROME: MYTH AND REALITY

The question of how Rome was founded has always been a place for speculations, legends, and rumors. According to legend, Rome was founded by Romulus, a descendant of the Troyan Aeneas. In reality, multiple small settlements, situated in a strategic position on the hills overlooking the Tiber river, grew together and formed Rome. Let`s dive into the myth and the reality of how the eternal city of Rome originated.

Rome's founding legend

Due to a lack of concrete evidence regarding the founding of Rome, the Romans resorted to creating a myth that linked Rome with the Trojan War. The myth suggests that a Trojan named Aeneas, who happened to be the son of the goddess Venus, escaped the destruction of Troy along with his son Iulus. Interestingly, Julius Caesar claimed Iulus as the progenitor of the Julius clan, which gave him a direct connection to both the gods and the founding father of Rome.

Similar to the legendary Greek hero Odysseus, Aeneas and his companions were compelled to wander across the Mediterranean before ultimately settling in the region that would become modern-day Rome. Aeneas' son Iulus founded the city of Alba Longa around 1060 BC, which was ruled by his descendants for many centuries.

The last two kings of Alba Longa, Numitor and Amulius, were brothers. Numitor was the rightful king but was overthrown by his cruel and tyrannical brother, Amulius. In an attempt to end Numitor's bloodline, Amulius forced Numitor's daughter, Rea Silvia, to become a priestess of the goddess Vesta, a position that required her to remain a virgin. One night, Mars, the Roman god of war, visited Rea Silvia and impregnated her with twins, Romulus and Remus.

Amulius, their granduncle, was infuriated and ordered that the infants be thrown into the sea. Fortunately, they were placed in a basket and, through divine intervention, washed up on the shore.

At the shoreline, the twins were discovered and cared for by a wolf before being rescued and raised by the shepherd Faustulus. This is why there are many statues of the wolf and the two infants in Rome.

After overthrowing their greatuncle and restoring their grandfather Numitor as the rightful king of Alba Longa, Romulus and Remus set out to establish their own city and did not remain in Alba Longa for long.

After overthrowing their great-uncle and restoring their grandfather to the throne, Romulus and Remus decided to leave Alba Longa to start their own city. However, the brothers disagreed on the location of the new city and eventually Romulus killed Remus in a fit of rage. This act made Romulus the sole founder of the new city, which he named Rome in honor of himself.

Romulus, having killed his brother, sought to populate his city and thus turned Rome into a sanctuary for the oppressed and persecuted. He promised them a life of freedom. This asylum, as per legend, held great political significance in shaping Rome's self-image.

During debates among Roman senators about granting defeated former enemies Roman civil rights, the asylum was often cited as evidence that Romulus, the founder of Rome, intended for foreigners and former enemies to be integrated into Rome. This formula was believed to have played a significant role in Rome's success.

Numerous men, including criminals evading the law and escaped slaves, settled in Rome, taking advantage of the opportunity. One could argue that this resulted in an illustrious group of individuals. However, this social composition created a problem: there were hardly any women. In typical rustic Roman fashion, the solution was to abduct women from their neighboring people, the Sabines.

The early Romans invited their Sabine neighbors, along with their women, daughters, and mothers, to a feast. When their guests became intoxicated, they were expelled while the women were held back by the Romans and (forcefully) married to their kidnappers. Unsurprisingly, the Sabine men were unwilling to accept the abduction of their women. They armed themselves and marched towards the settlement that would later become Rome, leading to heavy fighting between the Romans and the Sabines.

ROMMIS

The conflict was resolved when the women, caught between their new husbands and their families of origin, intervened and forced a peace treaty.

After their conflict, the Romans and Sabines agreed to join forces, and the kingship of Rome was shared between Romulus, a Roman, and Titus Tatius, a Sabine king.

Romulus governed Rome for 38 years until 715 BC, during which he established the senate, organized the army, structured the population into curiae, and distinguished between patricians and plebeians. These accomplishments are attributed to him in the founding myth.

Although much of Romulus's story is shrouded in legend and mythology, he is still a significant figure in Roman history and mythology. His legacy as the founder of Rome and the creator of its institutions has endured for thousands of years.

Upon Romulus's death during a thunderstorm, his body disappeared, and he was believed to have been included in the world of the Roman gods. Interestingly, he was the first Roman ruler to be deified, a practice that would become quite common after (and including) the death of Julius Caesar.

Romulus was succeeded by six other kings, all of whom were portrayed in stereotypical ways. It is now widely accepted that Rome was not founded by a descendant of the son of the goddess Venus, as per the founding myth.

However, there are many discrepancies and inconsistencies in this story. For one, it is unlikely that the Romans would have allowed a Vestal Virgin to have children, as they were expected to remain celibate for the duration of their service. Additionally, the idea of being raised by a she-wolf is clearly a mythological element, and there is no evidence to suggest that it actually happened.

Another theory suggests that Rome was founded by the Etruscans, a powerful civilization that inhabited the region prior to the rise of the Roman Republic. According to this theory, the Etruscans established a settlement on the site of modern-day Rome, which was then taken over by the Romans at a later date. There is some archaeological evidence to support this theory, such as the remains of Etruscan tombs and other structures in the area.

Regardless of the true origins of Rome, there is no denying that it went on to become one of the most powerful and influential cities in the ancient world. The Roman Republic, which was established in 509 BCE, marked a significant turning point in Roman history. Under this system of government, power was divided between two consuls who were elected by the people. This allowed for a more democratic approach to governing than the previous monarchy, and paved the way for the development of the Roman Empire.

03

The Roman Republic: Government and Society

It's time to take a journey through the Republic of Rome and learn all about its government and society. The Roman Republic was a very special time in history, and it was a great power that lasted for centuries.

The Roman Republic began in 509 BC and lasted for about 500 years. It was a form of government where the people of Rome elected their leaders and had a say in how the government was run. This was different from the other societies of the time, which were ruled by kings.

The Roman Republic was divided into two parts: the Senate and the people. The Senate was made up of wealthy and powerful men who made laws and proposed laws to the people. The people of Rome elected their own leaders, called consuls, who served for one year. The consuls were responsible for carrying out the laws that the Senate proposed.

The Roman Republic also had a complex social system that was based on wealth and power. The people of Rome were divided into different classes, with the wealthy and powerful at the top and the poor at the bottom. The wealthy and powerful were usually the senators and the consuls, while the poor were the farmers, artisans, and merchants.

The Roman Republic was a great place for the arts and literature. Writers, poets, and sculptors flourished during this time, creating works that still inspire us today. Roman architecture was also impressive, with great monuments, public works, and even the Colosseum, which is still standing today.

The Roman Republic also had a strong military, which allowed it to conquer many different lands. The Romans managed to control much of Europe, the Middle East, and North Africa during their time.

What is the Roman Republic?

The Roman Republic was an ancient civilization that ruled the Mediterranean region for centuries. It was founded in 509 BC by the Romans, a group of Latin-speaking people who had settled in the area.

The Roman Republic was made up of two parts: the Senate and the People. The Senate was composed of wealthy, influential men who were elected by the people of Rome and were responsible for making laws and decisions on behalf of the people. The People were all citizens of Rome who elected representatives to the Senate and had the power to pass laws and vote on the Senate's decisions.

The Roman Republic was a very powerful country. It had a strong military that was able to conquer lands, a great legal system, and an efficient taxation system. Its system of government was based on a combination of elected officials and appointed advisors.

The Roman Republic also had a unique culture and society. Its citizens lived in large cities like Rome and were divided into classes. The upper classes had more power and wealth than the lower classes, but all citizens had certain rights and freedoms. The Roman Republic also had a complex religion that included gods, goddesses, and rituals.

The Roman Republic was eventually replaced by the Roman Empire in 27 BC. The Republic was a major influence on the development of Western civilization and its government, laws, and culture are still seen today. It is an important part of history and an example of how a society can be successful and last for centuries.

What makes the Roman Republic special?

The Roman Republic is one of the most influential political and social systems in history. It was a government that provided stability and prosperity, while protecting the rights and freedoms of its citizens. From the time of its founding in 509 BCE, the Roman Republic grew to be one of the most powerful empires of all time.

The Roman Republic was special in many ways. Most notably, it was a republic, meaning it was a government run by elected representatives of the people. This allowed for greater participation and freedom of the people in government, as well as more equitable laws and policies.

The Roman Republic also had a strong emphasis on education. Citizens were required to attend school, which provided them with the knowledge and skills to become active citizens. This education system gave the Roman Republic a strong foundation for its growth and success.

The Roman Republic also had a commitment to justice. Its courts were fair and impartial and its laws were written so that everyone was treated fairly and equally. This commitment to justice was a key part of the Roman Republic's success.

The Roman Republic also had a unique and influential taxation system. This system was designed to be equitable and to provide the government with the money it needed to operate. This taxation system was so successful that it was used by many other governments throughout the world.

Finally, the Roman Republic had a strong sense of citizenship. Citizens were expected to take part in the government and to be engaged in civic life. This sense of citizenship was an important part of the Roman Republic's success.

The Roman Republic was a powerful and influential political and social system. Its emphasis on education, justice, and citizenship provided a strong foundation for its success. Its unique and influential taxation system was used by many other governments throughout the world. All of these factors made the Roman Republic a special and influential system that has had a lasting impact on history.

The Basic Structure of the Roman Republic

The Roman Republic was a form of government in ancient Rome that lasted for over 500 years. It was a highly organized political system that was based on a system of checks and balances and was designed to ensure the rights of all citizens. The basic structure of the Roman Republic was composed of three branches: the Senate, the Magistrates, and the People.

The Senate was the most important branch of the Roman Republic. It was made up of 300 members who were elected by the people for life. These senators were responsible for passing laws, deciding how Rome should be governed, and providing advice to the other two branches of government.

The Magistrates were the government officials who were appointed by the Senate to oversee the day-to-day running of the Roman Republic. They were responsible for ensuring that the laws were enforced, collecting taxes, and maintaining order in Rome.

The People were the citizens of the Roman Republic. They were given the right to vote and could elect representatives to the Senate. They also had the right to participate in public meetings and trials.

The Roman Republic was a complex and powerful government system that was designed to ensure the rights of all citizens. It was a system that lasted for over 500 years and was based on a system of checks and balances. By understanding the basic structure of the Roman Republic, children can gain a better understanding of how governments work and the importance of preserving the rights of citizens.

The Three Branches of Government

The Roman Republic was a complex and powerful government that had three branches. These three branches were the executive, legislative, and judicial branches. Each branch had a specific role in the government, and each branch worked together to ensure the Roman Republic was successful.

The executive branch was responsible for carrying out the laws and policies of the Roman Republic. This branch was headed by two consuls, who were elected by the people every year. The consuls had the power to make decisions, appoint people to government positions, and oversee the army.

The legislative branch was responsible for making laws and defining the government's policies. This branch was made up of the Senate, which was made up of wealthy, powerful people. The Senate had the power to pass laws, declare war, and appoint people to government positions.

The judicial branch was responsible for interpreting the laws and deciding cases. This branch was made up of judges, who were appointed by the consuls. The judges had the power to decide cases, interpret the laws, and punish those who violated them.

The three branches of the Roman Republic worked together to ensure that the government ran smoothly and efficiently. The executive, legislative, and judicial branches were vital in the success of the Roman Republic and the stability of its government.

The Senate

The Senate was a key part of the Roman Republic. It was the most powerful institution in the Republic and served as the upper house of the legislative branch of the Roman government. The Senate was made up of the most influential and well-respected men in Rome.

The Senate was composed of 300 members, known as Senators. Senators were usually wealthy or politically influential Roman citizens. They were appointed by the Roman Consuls, the two most powerful officials in the Republic. Senators were expected to hold high moral standards and were expected to be knowledgeable about the laws and customs of the Roman Republic.

The Senate was responsible for passing laws and deciding on foreign policy. The Senate also had the power to declare war and ratify treaties. The Senators also had the power to impeach and convict officials of the Roman government.

The Senate also had an advisory role, providing advice and counsel to the Roman Consuls. It was also responsible for appointing magistrates and other important officials.

The Senate was the most influential body in the Roman Republic and had great power. They were the only ones with the power to declare war, ratify treaties, and impeach officials. It was the Senate that ultimately held the power to decide the fate of the Roman Republic.

The Senate was a powerful institution, and its members were expected to act with integrity and uphold the highest moral standards. It was the Senate that ultimately held the power to determine the fate of the Roman Republic.

The Magistrates

The Magistrates of the Roman Republic were an integral part of the government and society. They were government officials who were elected by the people to serve the republic and its citizens. Magistrates were responsible for overseeing the laws and regulations of the Republic, as well as administering justice and managing the day-to-day affairs of the Republic.

Magistrates were elected for a one-year term, but could be re-elected if they were successful in their first term. The election was done by the people and the most popular candidates were usually elected. To be eligible to become a magistrate, a citizen had to be an adult male, a Roman citizen, and have a certain amount of wealth.

Magistrates had a variety of duties and responsibilities. They were responsible for law enforcement, taxation, public works projects, and other municipal tasks. They also had the power to declare war, ratify treaties, and pass laws. Magistrates also had the authority to pass sentence on criminals and preside over legal disputes.

The highest ranking magistrates were known as the "consuls". There were two consuls at any given time, and they were the main representatives of the government. They had the power to preside over the Senate, and had the authority to veto any law proposed by the Senate.

Magistrates were also responsible for managing the military. They had the power to appoint military commanders, organize the military forces, and lead them in battle. Magistrates were also responsible for organizing public festivals and religious ceremonies.

The magistrates were part of a system of checks and balances that kept the Republic functioning. They were an essential part of the Roman Republic's government and society, and their role was vital to its success.

The Assemblies

The Assemblies of the Roman Republic were the foundations of the Roman government. They were the main source of political power and decisions in the Republic. It was through the Assemblies that the Roman people elected their leaders, made laws, and declared war.

The Roman Assemblies were divided into two main types: the Centuriate Assembly and the Tribal Assembly. The Centuriate Assembly was made up of all citizens who held a certain property qualification. This Assembly voted on matters such as the election of magistrates, the passing of laws, and the declaration of war. The Tribal Assembly was composed of all citizens, regardless of their property qualification. This Assembly voted on matters such as the election of magistrates, the repeal of laws, and the confirmation of laws passed by the Centuriate Assembly.

The Centuriate Assembly was the most powerful Assembly in the Roman Republic. It was made up of 193 centuries, or voting blocks, of citizens. Each century was divided into three classes based on wealth. The wealthiest citizens were placed in the first class and voted first. The Tribal Assembly was composed of 35 voting blocks of citizens.

The Assemblies had the power to elect the Roman magistrates, approve new laws, and declare war. The election of magistrates was done by a voting system called the comitia centuriata. This system allowed the citizens to choose their magistrates from among the candidates. The Assemblies also had the power to approve new laws, which were called plebiscites. Finally, the Assemblies had the power to declare war, which was done through a process known as the bellum iustum.

The Assemblies of the Roman Republic were the basis of the Roman government. They were the main source of political power and decisions in the Republic. Through the Assemblies, the Roman people elected their leaders, made laws, and declared war.

How the Three Branches Work Together

The Roman Republic was a complex and highly organized government system. At the heart of it was the three branches of government: the Senate, the Assembly, and the Magistrates. Each branch had its own unique responsibilities and worked together to form the backbone of the Republic.

The Senate was the most powerful branch of government and was made up of the wealthy and powerful patricians. This branch was responsible for making laws and debating important issues. The Assembly was comprised of elected representatives from all Roman citizens and was responsible for voting on laws and electing magistrates.

The Magistrates were the elected officials who were responsible for carrying out the laws and executing justice. They could issue decrees, act as judges in court, and even declare war. Magistrates were elected by the Assembly and served for a period of one year.

The three branches worked together to ensure the Republic ran smoothly. The Senate would debate important matters and pass laws that the Assembly would then vote on. The Assembly would elect magistrates to carry out the laws and ensure justice was served.

By working together, the three branches of government provided the Roman Republic with a strong and stable government system that lasted for centuries. They ensured that the Republic was run fairly, efficiently, and effectively. The Romans understood the importance of each branch and worked to ensure that all three branches worked together for the benefit of the Republic.

Roman Society

Roman Society was an incredibly important part of the Roman Republic. During the time of the Republic, Rome was a city-state with a large population of citizens, equites (upper class citizens), and slaves. Roman society was divided into two main classes: patricians and plebeians.

The patricians were the most powerful and wealthy members of society. They were the ruling class and held all the political power in the government. They owned the vast majority of land and were the only citizens allowed to become senators.

The plebeians were the lower class citizens. They were farmers, merchants, laborers, and artisans. They had some rights under the law, but were not allowed to hold political office or own large amounts of land.

The Roman Republic was a complex system of social stratification. The citizens of Rome were divided into distinct social classes, each with its own privileges and responsibilities. The citizens of Rome were expected to adhere to the laws and customs of their social class.

The equites were the upper class citizens of Rome. They were wealthy and influential, but were still limited in their political power. They were able to vote in the assemblies, but were not allowed to run for office.

The slaves were the lowest class of citizens in Roman society. They had no rights and were considered property. Slaves could be bought and sold and were used for labor in the fields and homes.

Roman society was a highly structured system that regulated the behavior of citizens. It was based on the rule of law and was designed to maintain the stability of the Republic. Despite its rigid social structure, Roman society was highly successful and lasted for centuries.

Slavery in the Roman Republic

Slavery was an important part of the Roman Republic. Slaves were people who were owned by others and had no rights or freedom. They were used to do work that was too difficult or unpleasant for free citizens. Slaves in the Roman Republic could be bought and sold, and were used to do a wide variety of jobs.

Slaves were used in the homes of wealthy families to do domestic work, such as cooking, cleaning, and looking after children. They were also employed in factories, mines, and fields. Slaves were mainly used to grow food and make clothing. They were also used in the military, where they served as servants, cooks, and artisans.

Slaves in the Roman Republic usually came from other countries, especially those conquered by the Romans. They were also bought on the open market, or captured during wars. Some slaves were born in the Republic, but their freedom was taken away if their parents were slaves.

Slaves had no rights in the Roman Republic. They were not allowed to be educated, marry, or own property. They were treated as property, and could be punished or even killed by their owners without legal consequence. It was not uncommon for slaves to be branded or have their limbs amputated as punishment.

Despite the harsh treatment, some slaves were able to gain their freedom. They could be freed by their owners, or they could buy their own freedom with money they had saved. Once freed, former slaves were known in Roman society as "freedmen", and had more rights than slaves.

Slavery was an important part of the Roman Republic, but it was also seen as a necessary evil. Slaves were a valuable source of labor and enabled the Republic to thrive. It was a controversial subject, and some people argued that it was wrong and should be abolished. Although slavery was eventually abolished in the Roman Republic, it had a lasting impact on society.

Roman Festivals

Roman Festivals were among the most important cultural events of the Roman Republic. They were an opportunity to celebrate gods, honor ancestors, and show loyalty to the state. Most Roman festivals were religious in nature, and many were held in honor of the gods and goddesses of Rome. The most important festivals were the Saturnalia, Ludi Magni, and the Lupercalia.

The Saturnalia was a week-long celebration of the god Saturn that was held in December. During the Saturnalia, the laws of Rome were suspended and people could do whatever they wanted. This included giving gifts and feasts, playing games, and dressing up in special clothes.

The Ludi Magni was a series of games and rituals held in honor of Jupiter, the most powerful Roman god. The games included chariot racing, wrestling, and theatrical performances. This festival was held in July and August and was the highlight of the Roman social calendar.

The Lupercalia was a fertility festival that honored the god Faunus and the goddesses Juno and Fortuna. During the festival, men would run around Rome naked and whip women with straps. It was believed that this would help the women become fertile. The Lupercalia was celebrated in February.

Roman festivals were an important part of the Roman Republic's culture and society. They were a way for people to honor their gods and celebrate their loyalty to Rome. Even today, many of the festivals are still celebrated in some form or another.

04

THE GLADIATORS

Who were the Gladiators?

The Gladiators were some of the most famous people of the Roman Empire. They were trained warriors who fought each other in the arenas for the entertainment of the Roman public. Gladiators were usually slaves, prisoners of war, or criminals who had been sentenced to fight in the arena. Gladiators were seen as symbols of bravery and strength, and the Roman people often cheered for their favorite gladiators.

Gladiators were divided into different classes based on their weapons and armor. There were Thracian gladiators who used a curved sword and a small round shield, and Samnite gladiators who wore a helmet, a shield, and a sword. Other types of gladiators included the Retiarius, who used a net and a trident, and the Hoplomachus, who wore a helmet, a shield, and a spear.

Gladiators were trained in special schools called 'ludi', and they had to follow strict rules and training regimens. The gladiators would fight each other in the arena, and the winner was usually decided by a referee. Some gladiators were even given special awards, such as a golden crown or a wooden staff.

Gladiatorial fights could be very dangerous, and often ended in death. However, the gladiators were often praised for their courage and strength, and some became famous and beloved by the Roman people. Gladiators were seen as heroes, and some even had statues built in their honor.

Gladiators were an important part of the Roman Empire, and their legacy still lives on today. While the gladiatorial games ended long ago, their memory still remains. The gladiators of the Roman Empire were true warriors, and their courage and skill will always be remembered.

Why were Gladiators Popular?

Gladiator fights were popular in the Roman Empire for many reasons. The first and most obvious is that people liked to watch them. Gladiators were skilled fighters and put on dramatic and exciting shows for the crowd. People enjoyed watching the gladiators compete against each other and were often willing to bet on the outcome.

Another reason gladiators were popular is because they were seen as heroes and symbols of strength and courage. Gladiators had to go through rigorous training and preparation before they could fight in the arena. They were admired by the public for their bravery and skill.

Gladiators also provided entertainment to the Roman people. The Roman people enjoyed watching gladiators fight, but they also liked to watch animal fights. Gladiators would often fight against animals such as lions and bears. This was a popular form of entertainment for the Romans and helped to keep them entertained.

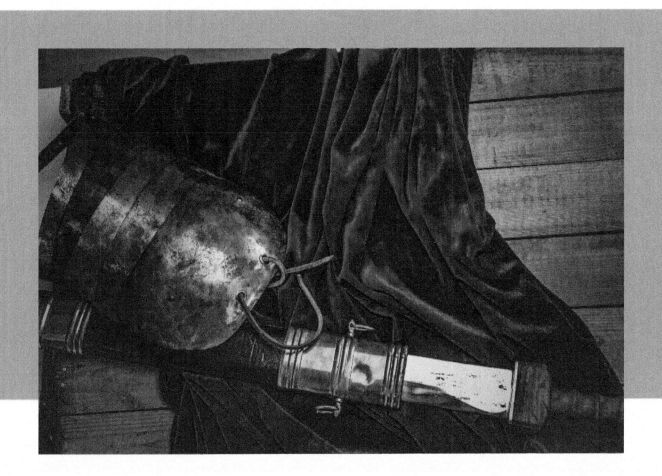

Finally, gladiators served an important role in Roman society. Gladiators were used as a form of punishment for criminals and slaves. They were also used in military training and to discourage people from rebelling against the Roman government. This was a way for the government to maintain control over its people.

Gladiators were popular in the Roman Empire for many reasons. They were skilled fighters who put on exciting shows for the crowd, they were admired as heroes and symbols of strength, they provided entertainment to the Roman people, and they served an important role in Roman society.

What was a Gladiator's Life Like?

Life as a gladiator was harsh, violent, and often short. Gladiators were slaves or prisoners of war forced to fight for the amusement of the Roman people. They lived in cramped cells, were fed a meager diet, and were trained to fight with a variety of weapons.

Life in the arena was even more dangerous. Gladiators fought one another, wild animals, and even condemned criminals in contests watched by thousands of spectators. Even if they won, they were often injured or killed in battle.

Gladiators were divided into different classes with different types of weapons, armor, and fighting styles. The most popular gladiators were the Samnites, who fought with shields, swords, and helmets. The Retiarii fought with tridents and nets, while the Murmillones used swords and small shields.

The life of a gladiator was not all fighting. They were highly prized commodities and were sometimes even taken on tours around the empire to give exhibitions of their fighting skills. Gladiators also had privileges such as the ability to own property, marry, and even gain their freedom if they earned enough money from their battles.

Although life as a gladiator was brutal and often short, some gladiators achieved great fame and wealth. People like Spartacus, Crixus, and Heracles achieved legendary status and even became symbols of Roman culture and power.

Gladiators were a reminder of the harsh and violent world of the Roman Empire. They were a symbol of the power of the Roman people and their ability to bring life and death to the arena.

05

THE ROMAN EMPERORS

Julius Caesar

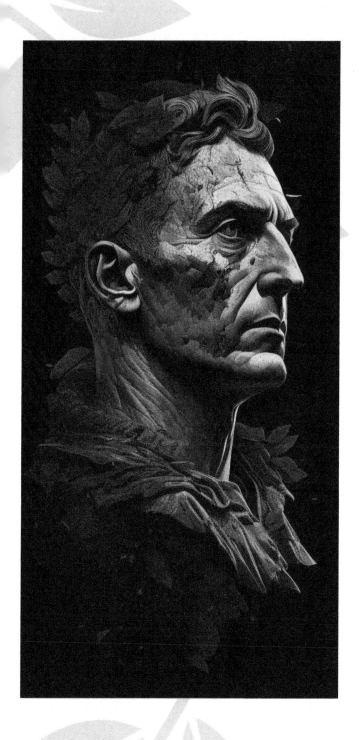

Julius Caesar was one of the most famous figures of Ancient Rome. He was a great military leader and statesman, and his life story is full of adventure and intrigue.

Caesar was born in 100 BC, and his family was aristocratic but not especially wealthy. He was educated in Latin and Greek, and developed his skills as a speaker and writer. Caesar began his career in the Roman military, leading successful campaigns in Spain and Gaul (modern day France).

In 59 BC, Caesar became a consul, the most powerful position in the Roman Republic. He then embarked on a campaign of reforms, which brought him into conflict with the Senate, the ruling body of the Republic. In 49 BC, he crossed the Rubicon river and declared civil war against the Senate. After almost a decade of war, Caesar emerged triumphant in 44 BC, and he was made dictator for life.

As dictator, Caesar continued his reforms, and he even tried to introduce his own calendar system. He was assassinated in 44 BC by a group of senators who feared his growing power. After his death, his adopted son, Octavian, would become the first Emperor of Rome.

Julius Caesar changed the course of Roman history, and his life and legacy are still remembered today. He is considered one of the greatest military commanders of all time, and his story is an inspiration to all who seek power and success. To this day, the words "crossing the Rubicon" are used to describe any action that marks a dramatic change.

Augustus Caesar

Augustus Caesar was one of the most influential figures in the Roman Empire. He was born Gaius Octavius in 63 B.C., and was the adopted son of Julius Caesar. After Julius' assassination in 44 B.C., Augustus was adopted as his son and heir and took the name Augustus Caesar.

Augustus was the first Roman Emperor, and is seen as the founder of the Roman Empire. He was a great leader and a reformer who worked to bring peace and stability to the Empire. He also reformed the Roman government and military, promoted the arts, and built many public works projects.

Augustus was a strong military leader who conquered many new territories and brought peace to the Empire. He was a great diplomat as well, negotiating treaties and alliances with other nations. He also reformed the Roman army and navy, making them more efficient and powerful.

Augustus was also a great patron of the arts. He helped to revive and promote many aspects of Roman culture, including literature, poetry, sculpture, and architecture. He built and restored many famous monuments, including the Pantheon and the Forum of Augustus.

Augustus was a great ruler who was beloved by the people of the Roman Empire. He was a strong leader and reformer who brought peace and prosperity to the Empire. He is remembered as one of the greatest rulers of the Roman Empire and is still revered today.

Other Important Emperors

The Roman Empire was a huge and powerful political entity that lasted from 27 BC to 476 AD. It was a period of great advancement in terms of culture, art, and architecture, but it was also a period of great rulers – the Emperors. In this chapter, we will take a look at some of the other important Emperors who left their mark on the Roman Empire.

The first of these was Claudius, who was Emperor from 41 to 54 AD and is known for his many reforms and military conquests. He was the first Roman Emperor to invade Britain, and he also encouraged and promoted trade and commerce, as well as public works and infrastructure.

Another important emperor was Hadrian, who reigned from 117 to 138 AD and is known for his great building projects. He ordered the construction of the famous Hadrian's Wall between England and Scotland and also built a temple to Jupiter in the city of Rome. He also made the Pantheon, a temple dedicated to all the gods of Ancient Rome, and he is known for his many other public works and building projects.

Marcus Aurelius, who ruled from 161 to 180 AD, is another important Emperor. He is best known for his philosophical works, especially his book "Meditations", which is still read today. He was also a great military leader, expanding the Empire's borders and defending it from invasion.

The last great Emperor was Constantine the Great, who reigned from 306 to 337 AD. He was a major proponent of Christianity and is credited with making it the official religion of the Roman Empire. He also moved the capital of the Empire from Rome to Constantinople, which is now known as Istanbul and is the capital of Turkey.

These are just a few of the important Emperors who left their mark on the Roman Empire. Their legacy is still felt today, and they are remembered as some of the most powerful and influential leaders in the history of the world.

06

DAILY LIFE IN THE ROMAN EMPIRE

Religion

Religion played an important role in the Roman Empire. It was believed that the gods had the power to affect people's lives. Many of the gods were borrowed from the Greeks, but the Romans gave them different names.

The most important god in the Roman religion was Jupiter, the king of the gods. He was the god of the sky, thunder and lightning. He was in charge of the other gods and watched over the Roman Empire. He was often shown holding a lightning bolt in one hand.

The second most important god was Mars, the god of war. He was in charge of protecting the Roman Empire from their enemies. He was often shown wearing armor with a spear in his hand.

The goddess Juno was the wife of Jupiter. She was the goddess of marriage and family. She was also the protector of the Roman state. She was usually depicted with a peacock or a cow.

The goddess Minerva was the goddess of wisdom and learning. She was often shown with a helmet and a spear.

The god Neptune was the god of the sea. He was usually shown with a trident in his hand.

The god Apollo was the god of the sun and music. He was usually shown with a lyre in his hand.

The god Mercury was the messenger of the gods. He was usually shown with wings on his helmet and sandals.

The goddess Venus was the goddess of love and beauty. She was usually depicted with a bow and arrow.

The god Vulcan was the god of fire and the forge. He was usually shown with a hammer in his hand.

Romans believed that all of these gods had the power to affect their lives. They would offer sacrifices and prayers to the gods in hopes of getting good fortune and protection. Temples were built to honor the gods, and festivals were held in their honor.

The Romans also believed in the existence of many other gods and goddesses, such as Bacchus, the god of wine, or Ceres, the goddess of agriculture. There were also many other gods and goddesses that were not as well known.

Roman religion was complex and interesting. It was a central part of life in the Roman Empire and is still studied by historians today.

Education

Education was an important part of the Roman Empire, just like it is today. In the Roman Empire, children were taught to read, write, and do mathematics. However, education in the Roman Empire was not free. Wealthy families could afford to send their children to school and learn from tutors. Poorer families often could not afford to send their children to school, and instead, the children had to work to help support their families.

Schools in the Roman Empire were divided into two categories: elementary school and secondary school. Elementary school was open to all children, regardless of social status. At elementary school, children learned the basics of reading, writing, and mathematics.

Secondary school was for children from wealthier families. At secondary school, children studied more advanced topics in literature, philosophy, and science. Boys were the only ones allowed to attend secondary school, and girls were taught at home.

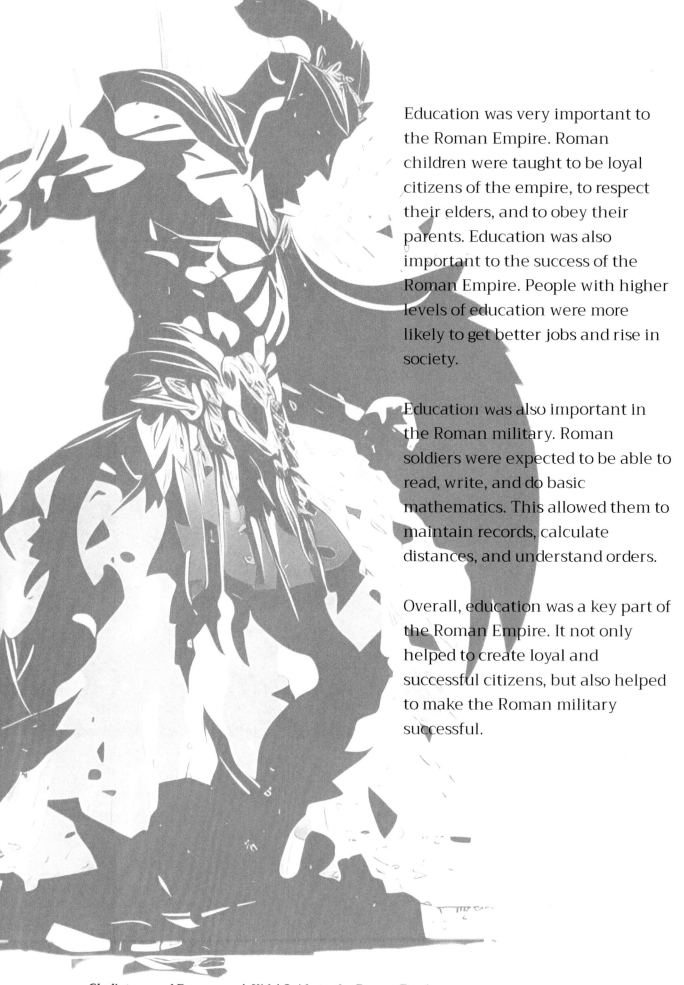

Education was very important to the Roman Empire. Roman children were taught to be loyal citizens of the empire, to respect their elders, and to obey their parents. Education was also important to the success of the Roman Empire. People with higher levels of education were more likely to get better jobs and rise in society.

Education was also important in the Roman military. Roman soldiers were expected to be able to read, write, and do basic mathematics. This allowed them to maintain records, calculate distances, and understand orders.

Overall, education was a key part of the Roman Empire. It not only helped to create loyal and successful citizens, but also helped to make the Roman military successful.

Entertainment

Entertainment was an important part of life in the Roman Empire. Gladiatorial contests were very popular with the Roman people. Gladiators were trained fighters who fought against each other or against wild animals in the arena. Sometimes the fights were to the death, although most of the time they were not. The most successful gladiators were honored with awards and could become very famous.

The Romans also enjoyed chariot races. Chariot teams were often sponsored by powerful Romans and the races were both exciting and dangerous. The drivers had to be skilled and brave to navigate their chariots around the track at high speeds.

The Romans also enjoyed theater. Plays were performed in large open-air theaters and often included comedy, drama, and music. Many of the plays were based on legends and myths from Roman history.

Another popular form of entertainment was the circus. Circuses featured performers such as acrobats, jugglers, and tightrope walkers. They also showcased exotic animals from all over the world, including lions, tigers, and elephants.

The Romans also enjoyed sports such as wrestling, boxing, and javelin throwing. They were also very fond of gambling, and many Romans spent their time in the gambling halls trying their luck.

Finally, the Romans enjoyed music and dancing. Musicians and dancers performed in the streets and in the homes of wealthy Romans. Roman music was often lively and energetic, and dancers often wore costumes and masks.

These activities were enjoyed by people of all classes and provided an escape from the everyday life of the Roman Empire. Entertainment was a vital part of life in the Roman Empire and it still influences us today.

07

THE ROMAN ARMY

Organization

Organization was a key factor in the success of the Roman Empire. The Romans had a very organized system of government, with an emperor at the head and a Senate, a body of elected representatives, to advise him. The Senate was made up of wealthy and powerful members of the Roman elite, and the emperor was the ultimate authority.

The army was also highly organized. It was divided into legions of about 5,000 soldiers, each commanded by a general. The Roman army was one of the most successful in history, conquering vast amounts of land and expanding the borders of the Roman Empire.

The Roman Empire was also divided into provinces, with each province ruled by a governor appointed by the emperor. These governors were responsible for raising taxes, collecting tribute, and keeping the peace. Each province was further divided into cities and towns, which were ruled by municipal magistrates.

The Roman government also had a system of laws, which were written down in the Codex Justinianus. This was a collection of Roman laws that were enforced by the courts.

The Roman Empire was a complex and well-organized society, and its success was built upon this organization. The emperor was the ultimate authority, and the Senate and army ensured that the laws were obeyed and that the citizens of the empire were kept safe. The provinces and cities were administered by governors and magistrates, and the laws were enforced by the courts. This structure enabled the Romans to maintain order and stability, and to build a powerful and prosperous empire.

Tactics

The Roman Empire was known for its military might and strategy. Roman tactics were among the most advanced of their time, allowing them to conquer and control vast swathes of Europe and beyond.

Roman tactics varied depending on the type of unit (infantry, cavalry, or other) and the type of battle being fought. Infantry tactics revolved around the use of the shield wall, a line of soldiers forming a tight defensive formation which could be used to repel enemy attacks. This shield wall could be moved forward or backward to gain an advantage over the enemy.

Cavalry tactics were more mobile, with Roman cavalry forming a loose line of riders which could be used to break up enemy formations or to outflank them. Cavalry units could also be used to sneak behind enemy lines and launch surprise attacks.

Roman tactics also included the use of siege engines, such as catapults, ballistae, and battering rams, to breach enemy fortifications, as well as advanced tactics such as the feigned retreat, where troops would retreat in an orderly fashion, only to turn and attack the pursuing enemy.

Roman tactics also included the use of psychological warfare, such as intimidating the enemy with their discipline and ferocity. Roman legions could also be used to intimidate potential enemies by marching through their territory or by sending a message of terror.

These tactics allowed the Romans to conquer and control vast swathes of Europe and beyond, and gave them a formidable reputation as one of the most advanced and powerful military forces of their time.

Equipment

The Roman gladiator was a fierce warrior, ready to battle for his life in the arena. To do so, he needed the right equipment.

The gladiator's weapons often included a sword, a shield, and a spear. He could wear armor to protect himself from his opponent's blows. Depending on the type of gladiator, he could also wear a helmet and greaves to protect his head and legs.

The shield was the gladiator's primary defense. It was usually made of wood, covered in leather and metal. It had a round shape and was large enough to cover the gladiator's body. The shield had a curved handle at the back, so he could hold it up and use it to block his opponent's sword.

The sword was the gladiator's main weapon. It was usually made of iron and was curved and pointed at the end. It measured about two feet in length and was used for thrusting and cutting.

The spear was a longer weapon, measuring about five or six feet in length. It was made of iron and had a sharp point at the end. It was used to thrust and stab at an opponent.

The armor the gladiator wore was often made of metal and leather. It was designed to protect the gladiator from his opponent's blows. Some gladiators also wore helmets, which were made of metal and had a crest on top. Greaves were pieces of metal armor that covered the legs.

Finally, the gladiator could also carry a dagger or a trident. The dagger was a short weapon, made of metal, and was used for thrusting and cutting. The trident was a longer weapon, made of metal, with three sharp points at the end. It was used to thrust and hook the opponent's shield.

The equipment the gladiators used was essential for their survival in the arena. Without the right weapons and armor, the gladiators would have been at a great disadvantage against their opponents.

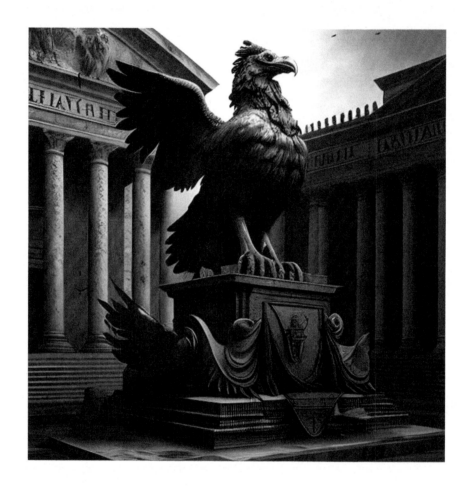

08

THE DECLINE OF THE ROMAN EMPIRE

Political Causes

When it comes to the Roman Empire, it is important to understand the political causes behind the rise and fall of this great civilization. The Roman Empire was a large and powerful state that controlled much of the Mediterranean region for centuries. In order to understand why the Roman Empire rose and eventually fell, it is important to look at the political causes that shaped its history.

One of the main political causes of the rise of the Roman Empire was the unification of Italy under the Roman Republic. The Roman Republic was a government that unified much of the Italian peninsula, which allowed the Roman Empire to expand and become a powerful state. The Roman Republic was also successful in its military campaigns against other nations, which allowed it to expand its territory and influence.

The Roman Empire also gained strength and power through its political system. The Roman Empire had a strong monarchical and aristocratic system of government that allowed it to remain stable and powerful. This system of government allowed the Roman Empire to maintain its strong economy, which in turn allowed it to maintain its powerful military forces.

The Roman Empire also benefited from its strong and well-developed legal system. The Roman Empire had a strong system of laws that allowed it to maintain order and justice throughout its territories. This system of laws was based on ancient Roman principles, which helped to ensure fairness and equality under the law.

The Roman Empire was also able to maintain its power and influence through its diplomatic relations with other nations. The Roman Empire had strong diplomatic ties with other states in the Mediterranean and beyond. This allowed the Roman Empire to remain influential and powerful, even when it was facing threats from other empires.

These are just some of the political causes that helped shape the Roman Empire. Understanding the political causes of the rise and fall of the Roman Empire is essential for understanding its history and its legacy.

Economic Causes

The Roman Empire was one of the most powerful empires in history, and its economic success was a major factor in its success. The Roman economy was based on agriculture and trade. As the empire grew, it developed a complex system of trade and taxation that allowed it to collect vast amounts of wealth and resources.

Agriculture was the main source of wealth in the Roman Empire. The Romans developed a sophisticated system of crop rotation and irrigation to maximize the productivity of their farms. They also developed a system of taxation that allowed them to collect money from the people in the provinces. This money was used to pay for public works such as roads, aqueducts, and public buildings.

The Romans also developed a sophisticated system of manufacturing and trade. They traded goods with the other empires in the Mediterranean, such as Egypt and Greece. They also exported goods to other parts of the world, such as Britain and India. The wealth generated by these trades was used to fund the military and public works of the Roman Empire.

In addition to agriculture and trade, the Roman Empire also relied heavily on slavery to power its economy. Slaves were used to work in the fields, build public works, and work in factories. This cheap labor allowed the Roman Empire to generate huge amounts of wealth, which it used to build its military and public works.

The economic success of the Roman Empire was a major factor in its success. The wealth generated by its agricultural and trade activities allowed it to build a powerful military and public works. The use of slavery to power its economy also allowed it to generate huge amounts of wealth, which it used to fund its military and public works. These economic factors allowed the Roman Empire to become one of the most powerful empires in history.

Social Causes

The Roman Empire was a vast and powerful empire that stretched across Europe and the Mediterranean. During its time, it was one of the most influential and powerful civilizations in history. As such, its citizens were subject to a myriad of social causes.

One of the most glaring social causes in the Roman Empire was the role of slavery. Slavery was a common practice in the ancient world, and the Romans were no exception. Slaves were used as laborers and servants, and were often owned by wealthy patrician families. Slaves were subject to harsh treatment and could be punished severely for minor offenses.

Another major social cause in the Roman Empire was the unequal treatment of women. Women were viewed as second-class citizens, and had very few legal rights. They could not own property, vote, or make decisions about their own lives. Marriage was also seen as a way for men to control women, and arranged marriages were common.

In addition to slavery and the unequal treatment of women, the social causes in the Roman Empire included public violence, poverty, and the lack of education. Public violence was a common problem, with street fights and riots common occurrences. Poverty was widespread, with many citizens living in abject conditions. Education was also limited, and only wealthy families could afford to send their children to school.

The social causes of the Roman Empire had a profound effect on its citizens, and these issues still resonate today. The Roman Empire was a complex civilization, and its citizens were subject to a myriad of social issues. These issues had a lasting impact on its citizens and the world we live in today.

09

THE LEGACY OF THE ROMAN EMPIRE

Architecture

The architecture of the Roman Empire was one of the most impressive in the ancient world. It was characterized by grandiose monuments, such as the Colosseum, the Pantheon, and the Forum Romanum. The Romans also built aqueducts to move water from one place to another, and roads to help them move their armies quickly and efficiently.

The Romans used a combination of stone and concrete in their architecture. They also used a type of concrete called pozzolana, which was made of volcanic ash and lime. This type of concrete was very strong and durable, and was used to build large monuments and public baths.

Roman architecture was heavily influenced by the Greeks and Etruscans, and was often adorned with decorations such as columns, arches, and sculpted statues. The most common type of column used by the Romans was the Corinthian column, which featured intricate carvings and decorations. The Romans also used arches to create grand entrances and doorways.

Roman roads were incredibly advanced for the time, and were built to last. They were typically built with a strong foundation of stones and gravel and were wide enough to accommodate two-way traffic. The Romans even built bridges to span rivers and valleys.

The Roman aqueducts were a marvel of engineering. They were built to carry water from one place to another, usually from a mountain spring to a large city. The aqueducts were built on an incline, so that gravity could help move the water.

The Colosseum was the most impressive monument built by the Romans. It was a huge amphitheater and could seat up to 50,000 people. It was used for gladiator fights, chariot races, and public executions.

The Roman Empire was a vast and powerful empire with stunning architecture. From monuments to aqueducts to roads, the Romans were able to create impressive structures that have stood the test of time. Today, many of these structures still stand, and are a testament to the engineering genius of the Roman Empire.

Language

Language is an important part of any culture and the Roman Empire was no exception. The Latin language was the official language of Rome and it was spoken by the ancient Romans. Latin was used in everyday life as well as in literature, law, and science. Latin was also used to communicate with other cultures, including those of the Greeks, Egyptians, and other cultures throughout the Mediterranean region.

In addition to Latin, the ancient Romans also spoke several other languages. Greek was the language of the educated elite and was spoken throughout the Mediterranean region. It was also used for scientific, medical, and philosophical writing. Other languages spoken in the Roman Empire included Etruscan, Egyptian, Phoenician, and Aramaic.

Latin was the language of the Roman Empire for centuries and it continues to influence modern languages. Many English words have Latin roots, such as "aqua" (water), "annus" (year), and "verbum" (word). Latin also had a major impact on the Romance languages, such as French, Spanish, and Italian.

The Latin language was also important in the development of literature. Roman poets, such as Virgil and Horace, wrote in Latin and their works are still read today. Latin was also used in the writing of history, philosophy, law, and science. It is easy to see why Latin was so important to the Roman Empire.

Today, Latin is still used in the Roman Catholic Church and in scientific and legal terminology. Latin is also used in the International Phonetic Alphabet and is a popular language for the study of history and the classics.

In conclusion, the Latin language was an important part of the Roman Empire and its influence can still be seen today. It was used for everyday communication, literature, law, science, and history. Latin had a major impact on modern languages and continues to be an important part of the Roman Catholic Church.

Religion

Religion was an important part of life in the Roman Empire. The Romans believed in a variety of gods and goddesses. The most important gods were Jupiter, the king of the gods, his wife Juno, and Minerva, the goddess of wisdom. Other gods included Mars, the god of war, and Mercury, the messenger of the gods. People in the Roman Empire also worshipped their ancestors and believed in spirits called numina.

The Romans had many festivals and holidays to honor their gods. The most important of these was the Saturnalia, a week-long celebration of the god Saturn. During this time, people decorated their homes, exchanged gifts, and held feasts. Other festivals included the Lupercalia, during which people sacrificed goats and dogs to honor the gods, and the Festival of Floralia, a spring celebration honoring the goddess Flora.

Religion also had a big influence on Roman law. The Roman Senate passed laws that regulated religious life, such as the Lex Sacrata, which limited the number of sacrifices that could be made. The Lex Aelia Sentia also required that slaves be given the same religious rights as free citizens.

Religious rituals were important for the Romans. They held ceremonies to honor their gods and goddesses. They made sacrifices of animals and food, and offered prayers to their gods. They also had special rituals for special occasions, such as the birth of a child or the dedication of a new temple.

Religion was also important in Roman politics. The most powerful people in the empire were often the high priests, who advised the emperor on religious matters. They also had the power to declare or annul laws, and make treaties with foreign nations.

Religion was a major part of life in the Roman Empire, and its influence can still be seen today. From the festivals and holidays we celebrate, to the laws we live by, the religious beliefs and practices of the Romans still shape our lives.

10

CONCLUSI
ON

Summary of the Roman Empire

The Roman Empire was the largest and longest-lasting civilization in history. It began in the city-state of Rome in 753 BC and lasted until 476 AD, when it was divided into the Western Roman Empire and the Eastern Roman Empire. During its existence, the Roman Empire became a powerful and influential force in the world.

At its peak, the Roman Empire stretched from Scotland in the north, to the Sahara Desert in the south and from Britain in the west to the Persian Empire in the east. It was made up of hundreds of provinces and cities, each with their own customs, laws, and religions.

Rome was the center of the Roman Empire, and its people were known as Romans. Rome was a powerful and influential city, and it was home to many great leaders, such as Julius Caesar, who was the first emperor of Rome.

The Roman Empire was divided into two parts: the Senate and the Emperor. The Senate was a group of elected representatives from the Roman people, who made laws and provided advice to the Emperor. The Emperor had the ultimate power and could veto any decision made by the Senate.

The Roman Empire was known for its powerful military and its engineering achievements. The Romans built roads, aqueducts, and many other structures to help them in their conquest and to maintain power. They also developed a form of writing called Latin, which is still used today.

The Roman Empire also had a rich culture, which was reflected in its art, literature, and religion. The most popular gods in the Roman Empire were Jupiter, the god of the sky, and Mars, the god of war.

The Roman Empire eventually fell in 476 AD, when it was invaded by the Visigoths. After the fall of the Roman Empire, the Western Roman Empire split into many different kingdoms, while the Eastern Roman Empire became what is known today as the Byzantine Empire.

Although the Roman Empire is no longer in existence, its legacy lives on in many ways. Its culture and its innovations have shaped the world we live in today.

What We Can Learn From the Roman Empire

The Roman Empire was one of the most powerful empires in the world and its influence is still seen today. But what can kids learn from the Roman Empire?

First, they can learn about the importance of a strong leader. The Roman Empire was run by a powerful emperor who made sure that everyone followed the laws and regulations. This was done to keep the empire stable and strong.

Second, kids can learn about the importance of having a strong military. The Roman Empire had one of the strongest armies in the world and was able to conquer many lands. This is why it was able to stay in power for so long.

Third, kids can learn about the importance of a strong economy. The Roman Empire had a very strong economy and was able to finance its military and other projects. This is why the Roman Empire was able to build great monuments and roads.

Fourth, kids can learn about the importance of architecture. The Roman Empire was known for its beautiful architecture and art that lasted for centuries. This is why many of the monuments and buildings from the Roman Empire are still standing today.

Finally, kids can learn about the importance of culture. The Roman Empire was very influential in spreading culture and art around the world. This is why many of the traditions and customs we use today came from the Roman Empire.

The Roman Empire was a powerful empire that left a lasting legacy. Kids can learn a lot from the Roman Empire and all the things it did. From a strong leader to a strong economy, to beautiful architecture and culture, kids can learn a lot from the Roman Empire and its impact on the world.

What We Can Do to Continue the Legacy of the Roman Empire

The Roman Empire is one of the most powerful and influential empires in history. Its legacy has been felt throughout the centuries, from its government and laws to its art and architecture. As kids, it can be difficult to understand the lasting impact of the Roman Empire, but it is important to remember that its legacy is still alive today.

One way to appreciate the legacy of the Roman Empire is to learn about its history. Reading books and articles about the Roman Empire can help kids better understand the events and people that contributed to its success. It can also help kids develop an appreciation for the culture and achievements that made the Roman Empire so influential.

Another way to continue the legacy of the Roman Empire is to visit its historical sites. Visiting ruins, museums and other locations that provide insight into the Roman Empire can help kids gain a better understanding of the empire's impact. Visiting these sites can also provide a great opportunity to learn about the different aspects of the Roman Empire and its influence on our world today.

Learning a language of the Roman Empire is another way to continue its legacy. Latin was the official language of the Roman Empire, and is still used in many places today. Learning Latin can help kids understand the language that was used by the Romans and gain a deeper appreciation for the language's influence on our own.

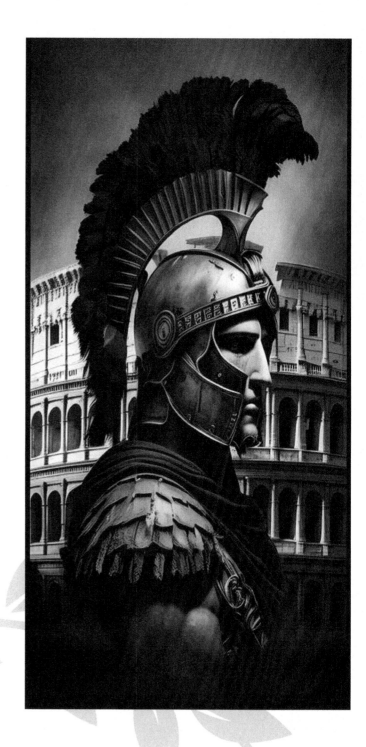

Finally, kids can continue the legacy of the Roman Empire by creating their own art and literature inspired by the Roman Empire. Whether it's creating a sculpture in the style of a classic Roman statue, writing a play in the style of a Roman comedy, or using ideas and concepts from the Roman Empire in their own artwork and writing, kids can find many ways to express their appreciation for the Roman Empire.

Bibliography

1. The History of the Roman Republic by Mary T. Boatwright. This comprehensive book provides a comprehensive overview of the Roman Republic, its government and society, and its legacy. It covers the founding of the Republic, the development of Roman law and religion, the rise of the Empire, and the decline of the Republic.

2. The Roman Republic: An Introduction by Robert T. Schulzinger. This book explores the social, political, and economic aspects of the Roman Republic and the ways in which it shaped the modern world. It also examines the impact of the Republic on other civilizations, including those of Greece, Egypt, and the Near East.

3. The Roman Republic: A Very Short Introduction by David L. Stone. This book provides an overview of the Roman Republic, its government, and its people. It covers the history of the Republic from its founding to its decline. It also looks at the impact of the Republic on other civilizations.

4. The Roman Empire: The Pros and Cons by Paul B. Harvey Jr. This book examines the strengths and weaknesses of the Roman Republic. It looks at the impact the Republic had on other civilizations, including those of Greece, Egypt, and the Near East.

5. The Roman Republic: A Sourcebook by Alan K. Bowman. This book provides a collection of primary sources relating to the Roman Republic, including texts, images, and artifacts. It is an excellent resource for anyone interested in learning more about the Republic, its government, and its people.

Printed in Great Britain
by Amazon

43916170R00044